W9-COH-567

AMAZING INVENTORS & INNOVATORS

ALEXANDER GRAHAM
BELL

LYNN DAVIS

Consulting Editor, Diane Craig, M.A./Reading Specialist

Super Sandcastle

An Imprint of Abdo Publishing
abdopublishing.com

abdopublishing.com

Published by Abdo Publishing, a division of ABDO, PO Box 398166, Minneapolis, Minnesota 55439.
Copyright © 2016 by Abdo Consulting Group, Inc. International copyrights reserved in all countries. No
part of this book may be reproduced in any form without written permission from the publisher. Super
SandCastle™ is a trademark and logo of Abdo Publishing.

Printed in the United States of America, North Mankato, Minnesota
062015
092015

THIS BOOK CONTAINS
RECYCLED MATERIALS

Editor: Liz Salzmann
Content Developer: Nancy Tuminelly
Cover and Interior Design and Production: Mighty Media, Inc.
Photo Credits: Library of Congress, Shutterstock, Wikicommons

Library of Congress Cataloging-in-Publication Data

Davis, Lynn, 1981- author.
Alexander Graham Bell / Lynn Davis ; consulting editor, Diane Craig, M.A./Reading Specialist.
     pages cm. -- (Amazing inventors & innovators)

Audience: K to grade 4
ISBN 978-1-62403-721-4

1. Bell, Alexander Graham, 1847-1922--Juvenile literature. 2. Inventors--United States--Biography--
Juvenile literature. 3. Telephone--United States--History--Juvenile literature. I. Title.

TK6143.B4D385 2016
621.385092--dc23
[B]
                              2014046603

Super SandCastle™ books are created by a team of professional educators, reading specialists, and
content developers around five essential components—phonemic awareness, phonics, vocabulary, text
comprehension, and fluency—to assist young readers as they develop reading skills and strategies and
increase their general knowledge. All books are written, reviewed, and leveled for guided reading, early
reading intervention, and Accelerated Reader™ programs for use in shared, guided, and independent
reading and writing activities to support a balanced approach to literacy instruction.

CONTENTS

ALEXANDER GRAHAM BELL

Alexander Graham Bell was an inventor. He invented the telephone. But first he was a teacher.

ALEXANDER GRAHAM BELL

BORN: March 3, 1847, Edinburgh, Scotland, United Kingdom

MARRIAGE: Mabel Hubbard, July 11, 1877, Cambridge, Massachusetts

CHILDREN: Elsie May, Marian, Edward, Robert

DIED: August 2, 1922, Beinn Bhreagh, Nova Scotia, Canada

A SOUND START

Alexander Graham Bell came from a family of public speakers. He learned to speak clearly at a young age.

Bell (second from left) with his wife, parents, and children

His mother was almost **deaf**. Alexander talked right into her forehead. She could hear the **vibrations** made by his voice.

Bell's mother, Eliza Grace Symonds Bell

SPEECH TRICKS

Bell as a teenager

Alexander began to experiment with sound as a boy.

He and his brother made a robot head. It could say a few words.

Bell's older brother, Melville James Bell

SPEAK!

Alexander also trained his dog. The dog would growl. Then Alexander would move its mouth. It sounded like the dog could say, "How are you, Grandma?"

TEACHING DEAF PEOPLE

Bell's first job was teaching. He taught **deaf** people to speak. He even founded a school.

Bell with Helen Keller

Bell (top right) at the Pemberton Square School, 1871

But he gave up teaching. He wanted more time to do experiments.

Bell's Laboratory, Boston, Massachusetts

Bell (right) flying a tetrahedral kite

Bell's Hydrodome number 4

IMPROVING THE TELEGRAPH

First, Bell worked on the **telegraph**. He tried to make it better. He used metal **reeds** to make sounds.

Harmonic telegraph, Bell's telegraph sender and receiver

The sounds went over a **telegraph** wire. He hoped to send more than one message on the same wire.

Alexander Graham Bell

A MEETING OF MINDS

Thomas Watson

Bell met Thomas Watson. Watson helped Bell with experiments. They did more tests with metal **reeds**.

A **reed** picked up **vibrations** from human speech.
The vibrations went through the **telegraph** wire.

THE FIRST TELEPHONE

Bell and Watson made a new machine. It had a **membrane** that **vibrated**.

Thomas Watson

Bell and Watson went to different rooms. They could hear each other through the machine. But they couldn't understand what each other was saying.

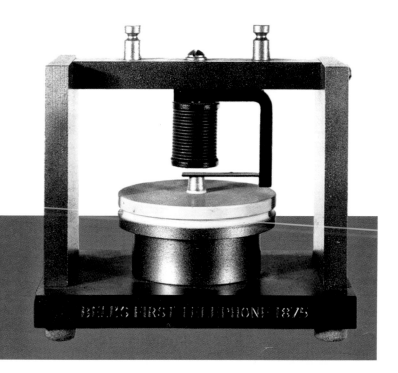

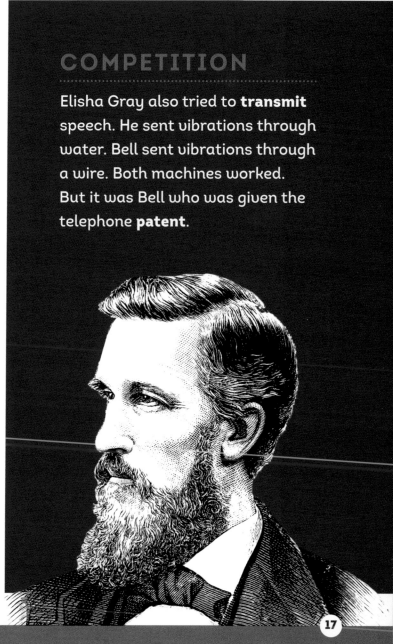

COMPETITION

Elisha Gray also tried to **transmit** speech. He sent vibrations through water. Bell sent vibrations through a wire. Both machines worked. But it was Bell who was given the telephone **patent**.

FUNNELING SOUND

A man with Bell's first telephone around 1920

Bell and Watson put a funnel right in front of the **membrane**. The funnel directed their speech onto the membrane.

They went into different rooms again. This time Bell and Watson could understand each other.

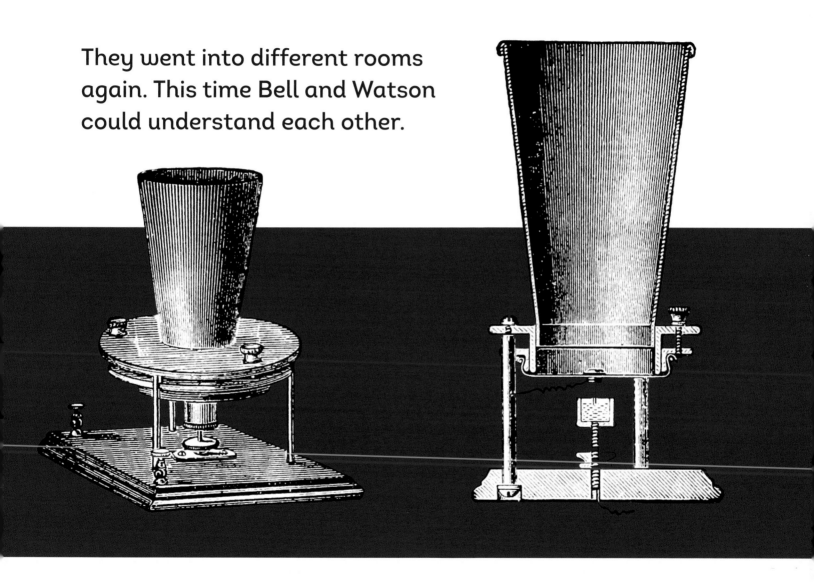

BELL'S SUCCESS

Many people had tried to make a machine that people could talk through.

Bell's big box telephone, one of the first sold, 1876

But Bell made the first telephone that worked!

Bell (center) in 1916

MORE ABOUT BELL

Bell invented the **PHOTOPHONE**. It sent a message on a beam of light. It didn't have wires.

Bell invented an early **METAL DETECTOR**.

Bell didn't want a telephone in his study. It **INTERRUPTED** his work.

TEST YOUR KNOWLEDGE

1. Bell's mother was almost **deaf**. True or false?

2. What was Bell's first job?

3. Who helped Bell make the telephone?

THINK ABOUT IT!

Who do you talk to on the telephone?

ANSWERS: 1. True 2. Teaching deaf people 3. Watson

GLOSSARY

deaf - unable to hear.

membrane - a thin, flexible sheet or layer, often made from animal skin.

patent - an official document giving one person the right to make, use, or sell an invention.

reed - a thin, flexible strip of wood, metal, or plastic.

telegraph - a machine that carries coded messages over wires.

transmit - to send through the air, water, or wires.

vibrate - to make very small, quick movements back and forth. The movements are called vibrations.